LANCASHIRE ONE HUNDRED YEARS AGO

Compiled by Frank Graham
From Old Prints

Jacket designed by Frank Varty

FRANK GRAHAM
6 Queen's Terrace, Newcastle upon Tyne, 2.

Published 1968

© 900409 81 9

Printed in Great Britain by Northumberland Press Ltd, Gateshead
Bound by Richard Clay (The Chaucer Press) Ltd, Bungay, Suffolk

FOREWORD

In the following pages we present a picture of Lancashire in the first half of the nineteenth century. We have used one hundred and forty-three old prints to show what the towns and villages of Lancashire were like in those days and have illustrated the castles and country houses when they were in a better state of preservation than they are today.

A little over a third of the prints are from *Lancashire Illustrated* which was published in 1832. This work was the most popular illustrated book on the county ever published and thousands of copies were sold. It was a fine production.

The second most important source of views is the *History of the County Palatine and Duchy of Lancaster* by Edward Baines, issued in 1836. This book has many fine views of country seats of which several were drawn by Thomas Allom.

Six of the finest full page views, including the jacket, have come from J. Corry's *History of Lancashire* (1832). *The Illustrated Itinerary of the County of Lancaster* (1842), Westall's *Great Britain Illustrated* (1829) and Harwood's *Scenery of Great Britain* have also been used.

Many of the small vignette views, especially those of Preston and district, were published by the famous London firm of Rock in the eighteen fifties. Some of the coastal views are from the well-known work *Finden's Views of the Ports, Harbours and Watering Places of Great Britain*, published in 1842 with drawings by W. H. Bartlett.

The remaining views are from a variety of sources. Most of the prints are reproduced in the same size as the original, but a few have been slightly reduced.

It will be noticed that some of the dates in the List of Plates do not coincide with the publication of the book from which they are taken. This is due to the fact that the prints were sometimes engraved a year or two earlier. Where the date is given on the print this is the one we have used.

LIST OF PLATES

Allom.

M. J. Starling

MARKET-STREET.—CUNLIFFES, BROOKS, & Cᵒ's BANK.

Harwood

F. J. Havell

MARKET STREET, FROM PICCADILLY, MANCHESTER.

MANCHESTER EXCHANGE.

Drawn & Engraved by James Barry for Corps. History of Lancashire

Drawn & Engraved by Ja.ᵗ Parry for Cerry's History of Lancashire

S.W. VIEW OF THE COLLEGIATE CHURCH TOWER MANCHESTER.

Harwood   F J Havell

MARKET STREET, FROM THE MARKET PLACE, MANCHESTER.

Harwood   M. J. Starling.

THE EXCHANGE, MANCHESTER.

THE COLLEGIATE CHURCH, MANCHESTER.

CHETHAM'S HOSPITAL, MANCHESTER.

Austin   McGahey

COTTON FACTORIES, UNION STREET, MANCHESTER.

Harwood   McGahey

THE TWIST FACTORY, OXFORD STREET, MANCHESTER.

GARRET-HALL, MANCHESTER.

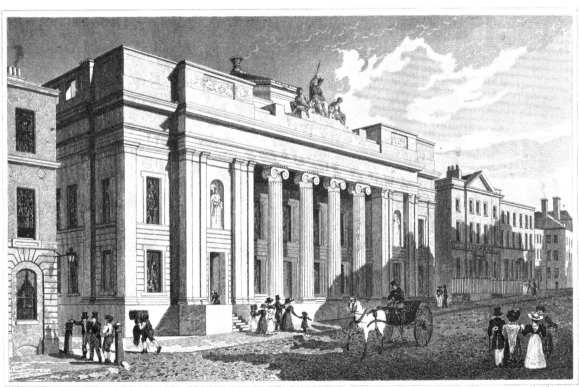

THE TOWN HALL, MANCHESTER.

MANCHESTER.

BLACKFRIARS BRIDGE, MANCHESTER.

Victoria Bridge, Manchester.

Mosley Street, Manchester.

Drawn by G. Pickering.

MANCHESTER.

Engraved by T. Higham.

Pl. no Vol. III.

Engraved by J. Walker from an Original Drawing by W. Orme. Publish'd Jan.ry 1.st 1797, by J. Walker N.o 16 Rosomans Street, London.

MANCHESTER.

MANCHESTER.

HULME HALL, NEAR MANCHESTER.

HULME-HALL, NEAR MANCHESTER.

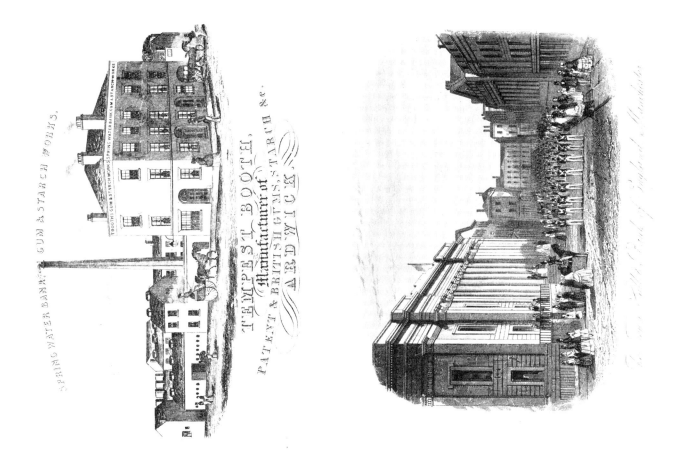

SPRING WATER BANK, GUM & STARCH WORKS.

TEMPEST BOOTH,
Manufacturer of
PATENT & BRITISH GUMS, STARCH &c.
ARDWICK.

Harwood

Watkins

ST. MATTHEW'S CHURCH, CAMP FIELD, MANCHESTER.

THE ROYAL INSTITUTION, MANCHESTER.

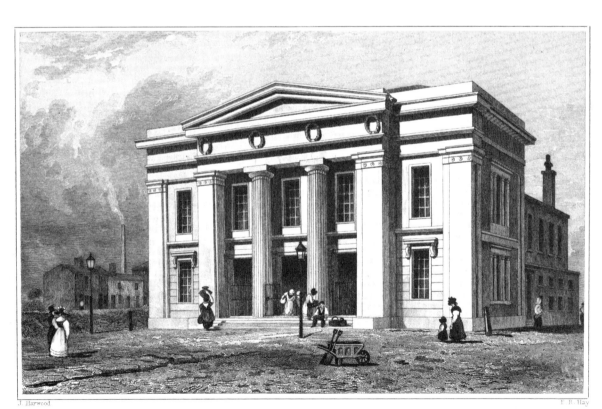

TOWN HALL, SALFORD.

A. Wilson, Pinxt.

Woodbury Process.

RURAL SPORT: OR A PEEP AT A LANCASHIRE RUSH-CART, 1821.

NEW JERUSALEM CHURCH, MANCHESTER.

Drawn by G. Pickering.

Engraved by J. H. Kernot.

SANKEY VIADUCT, LIVERPOOL & MANCHESTER RAIL-ROAD.

Drawn by T. Allom.

Engraved by R. Sands.

WORSLEY HALL, LANCASHIRE,

THE SEAT OF ROBERT HALDANE BRADSHAW, ESQ.

22

OLD HALL, OFFORD.

THE SEAT OF THOMAS HENRY CLARKE ESQ. DEP. LT.

Drawn by G. Pickering.

Engraved by W. Le Petit.

Drawn by G. Pickering.

Engraved by W. Le Petit.

TOWNELEY HALL.

23

Drawn by G. Pickering.   Engraved by C. Mottram.

BOLD HALL.

Drawn by T. Allom.   Sketched by J. Harwood.   Engraved by J. Sands.

WINWICK CHURCH.

24

WHALLEY ABBEY.

CROXTETH HALL.

WARRINGTON MARKET PLACE, LANCASHIRE.

WARRINGTON CHURCH, LANCASHIRE.

26

Seetzner del.

Pollard sculp.

VIEW OF ASHTON UNDER LINE.

ASHTON-UNDER-LINE, LANCASHIRE.

MARKET-PLACE, WIGAN, LANCASHIRE.

Dr. by G.P. C Pine.   Engraved by T. Aspland

HALE HALL.

Harwood.   De Petit.

FRIARS HALL, SHREWSBURY.

Harwood.   Watkins.

THE OLD MARKET PLACE, DEANSGATE, BOLTON.

Harwood.   Watkins.

STEAM-ENGINE MANUFACTORY, AND IRON-WORKS, BOLTON.

TO MESSRS. ROTHWELL, HICK & CO., THIS PLATE IS RESPECTFULLY INSCRIBED

BY THE PUBLISHERS.

FISHER, SON & CO. LONDON. 1828.

30

HALL I'TH' WOOD, NEAR BOLTON;
Where Mr Crompton constructed the first Spinning Mule

WHITE BULL INN, RIBCHESTER.

TURTON TOWER.

TOWNELEY HALL, VALE OF TODMORDEN, LANCASTER.

PRESTON.
FROM THE NORTH.

PRESTON, LANCASHIRE.

MARKET PLACE, PRESTON.

PRESTON, LANCASHIRE

Engraved by J. Walker, from an Original Drawing by W. Orme. _ Published Sep.1, 1796, by J. Walker N.16, Rosomans Street, London.

PRESTON.

Drawn by T. Allom. 7 Stories high-158 Y.ds long-18 Y.ds broad-660 Windows-37,500 Panes of Glass. Engraved by J. Tingle.

THE FACTORY OF MESS.RS SWAINSON, BIRLEY & C.O NEAR PRESTON, LANCASHIRE.

The Old Market Place, Preston

Barlington's Bull Hotel, Preston

Winckley Square, Preston

Town Hall, Preston

Park Parade & Avenham Walk, Preston

Bushell Place, Colonnade & Avenham Walk, Preston

Ashton Park, Preston

The Seat of Edward Pedder Esqr.

Penwortham, near Preston

Walton le dale, near Preston

View from Bushell Place & Avenham Walk, Preston

Penwortham Bridge, near Preston

Spa Springs Hotel & Baths, near Preston

Drawn from Nature by M.ʳ Pettiward

On Stone by H. James Jun.ʳ

WEST VIEW of TRAFFORD PARK the Seat of T. J. TRAFFORD ESQ.ᴿ,.

James Lithography, Manchester

39

HEALEY HALL, LANCASHIRE.

Engraved by Js. Palmer, for Corry's History of Lancashire.

40

SCAITCLIFFE

RED-SCAR,

Eng.d by James Tingle for Corry's History of Lancashire

THE GATE WAY TOWER OF LANCASTER CASTLE.

LANCASTER SESSIONS HOUSE AND MARKET.

LANCASTER CASTLE.

Lancaster

Engraved by A. Birrel, from a Painting by I. Ibbetson, in the possession of John Dent, Esq.r M.P. for Lancaster.   J. n. du.   for the Beauties of England & Wales.

LANCASTER,
View of the Church, Castle &c. from the S.E.

Painted by J. Henderson. Engraved by W. Hawkins.

LANCASTER.

Engraved by A. Walker from an Original Drawing by Dayes. Published Nov.ʳ 1.ˢᵗ 1797 by A. Walker, N.º 16 Rosomans Street, London.

LANCASTER.

Drawn by G. Pickering.

LANCASTER SANDS FROM HEST BANK.

Drawn on Stone by W Walton from a Sketch by Brian Gardner

Printed by Hullmandel

BRAMHALL OLD HALL.

BLACKPOOL SANDS.

Pub. 20. Oct.1781. by S.Hooper.

Kertmele Priory, Lancashire

Drawn by G & C. Pyne.   Engraved by L. Aspland.

SPEKE HALL.

Engraved by H. Meyer, for Corry's History of Lancashire.

A View of the Church of St Nicholas, Liverpool.

54

Drawn by Harwood.

Engraved by S. Winkles.

PART OF LORD STREET, WITH ST. GEORGE'S CHURCH IN THE DISTANCE.

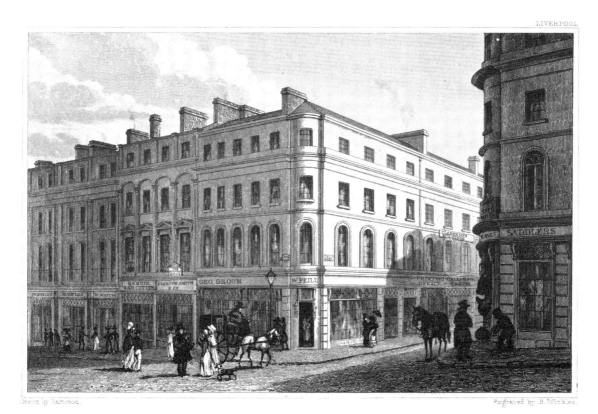

Drawn by Harwood.

Engraved by B. Winkles.

PART OF LORD STREET, AND SOUTH JOHN STREET.

Harwood   H Wallis

ST. GEORGE'S CRESCENT & CASTLE STREET.

Harwood.

LIVERPOOL FROM THE TOWN-HALL, LOOKING SOUTH.

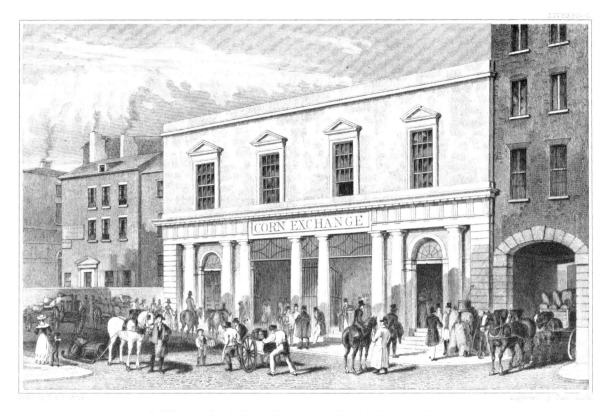

THE CORN EXCHANGE, BRUNSWICK STREET.

Drawn by G. & C. Pyne.   Engraved by Thos. Dixon.

EXCHANGE BUILDINGS AND NELSON'S MONUMENT.

ROYAL AMPHITHEATRE, LIVERPOOL.

N.W. VIEW OF ST. LUKE'S CHURCH, LIVERPOOL.

ST. JOHN'S MARKET, GREAT CHARLOTTE STREET, LIVERPOOL.

STATUE OF GEORGE III. LONDON ROAD.

Drawn by G.& C. Pyne.

Engraved by J. Starling.

ABERCROMBIE SQUARE.

Drawn by Thos Allom.

Engraved by Jas Allen.

THE INFIRMARY, BROWNLOW STREET.

WATER STREET

TOWN HALL, LIVERPOOL.

TOWN HALL AND MANSION HOUSE, LIVERPOOL.

Drawn by Samuel Austin.   Engraved by Robert Brandard

LIVERPOOL, FROM THE MERSEY, Nº I.

COMMENCING AT THE KEY DOCK TO THE NORTH

Drawn by Samuel Austin.   Engraved by Robert Brandard

LIVERPOOL, FROM THE MERSEY, Nº II.

COMMENCING AT THE PRINCE'S BASIN

LIVERPOOL, FROM THE MERSEY, N° III.

COMMENCING AT THE NEW BATHS KING GEORGE'S PARADE.

LIVERPOOL, FROM THE MERSEY, N° IV.

COMMENCING AT THE SHIP BUILDING YARDS, AND ENDING AT THE HERCULANEUM POTTERY.

"LIVERPOOL."

BLUE-COAT SCHOOL, LIVERPOOL.

THE ANCIENT HERRING-GATE, LIVERPOOL.

THE GOREE WAREHOUSES, GEORGE'S DOCK.

THE PRINCE'S DOCK, LIVERPOOL.

ST. NICHOLAS' CHURCH, LIVERPOOL.

(from St. George's Basin)

CANNING DOCK AND CUSTOM HOUSE, LIVERPOOL.

W. H. Bartlett.

J. C. Armytage.

THE STORM AT LIVERPOOL.

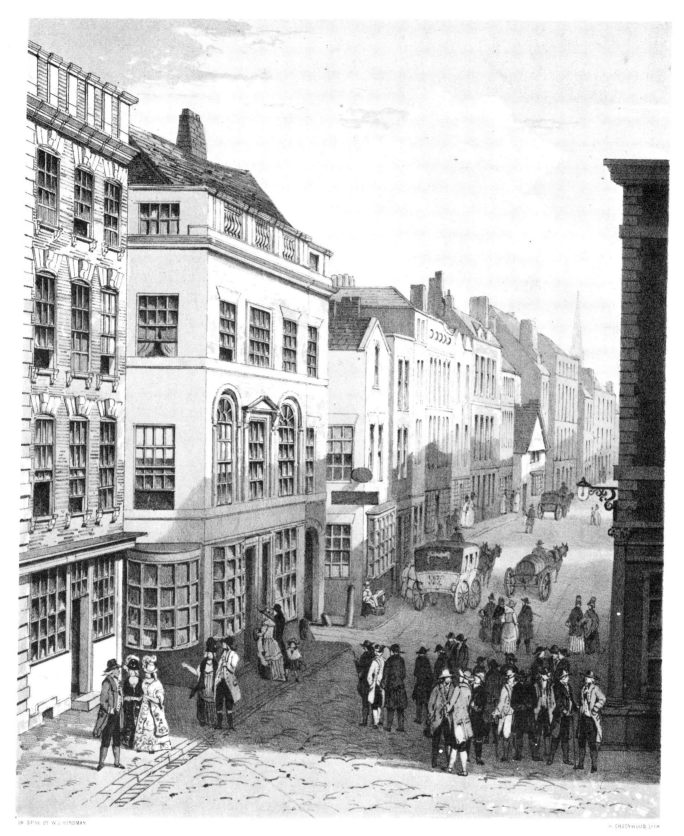

ON STONE BY W. G. HERDMAN

H. GREENWOOD, LITH

CASTLE STREET,
1786

KNOWSLEY HALL.

THE SEAT OF THE RIGHT HONOBLE THE EARL OF DERBY

HORNBY CASTLE.

HALTON HALL, NEAR LANCASTER.

Hoghton Towers, Lancashire (Entrance)

Hoghton Towers, Lancashire (Inner Court)

Wellington Hotels & Public Baths, Fleetwood

Worden Hall, Leyland, near Preston

The Seat of Mrs Farington

Town Hall, Southport, Lancashire

Promenade, Southport, Lancashire

ESTHWAITE WATER
From the Ulverston Road.

FURNESS ABBEY. SOUTH EAST.

CONISTON
from the wood above Bank ground

NEWBY BRIDGE

Ambleside Lake and Village of Lowwood, Westmoreland

Kirby Bridge
Lancaster

Drawn by T. Allom.   Engraved by W. Le Petit.

CONISTON WATER HEAD, NEAR COLTHOUSE, LANCASHIRE.

Drawn by G. Pickering.   Engraved by R. Sands.

ESTWAITE-WATER, LOOKING TOWARDS HAWKSHEAD.

78

MORECAMBE BAY & THE LAKE MOUNTAINS

Drawn & Engd by T. Allom & Son, R.A.

MORECAMBE

Bates & Co. Edin

Published by Thomas Hall & Co. Lancashire

CONISHEAD-PRIORY, NEAR ULVERSTON.

THE SEAT OF COL.^l BRADDYLL, TO WHOM THIS PLATE IS RESPECTFULLY DEDICATED,
BY THE PUBLISHERS.

Harwood

Bailey

Drawn by J. P. Neale.

Engraved by W. Radclyffe.

LATHOM HOUSE.